WUPATKI

AND

WALNUT CANYON

WUPATKI
And
WALNUT CANYON

New Perspectives on

History, Prehistory, and Rock Art

edited by

David Grant Noble

Ancient City Press
Santa Fe, New Mexico

For further information address: Ancient City Press, P.O. Box 5401, Santa Fe, New Mexico 87502. Telephone (505) 982-8195.

Cover photograph: Wupatki, photograph by David Grant Noble, 1992.

Frontispiece: San Francisco Peaks with Bonito Park in foreground. Photograph by George Huey, 1986.

Photograph, table of contents page: Box Canyon Ruin with San Francisco Peaks in background. Photograph by George Huey, 1986.

Cover design: Mary Powell

First Ancient City Press edition

International Standard Book Number: 0-941270-75-0

Library of Congress Catalog Number: 92-055034

10   9   8   7   6   5   4   3   2   1

Contents

THE SINAGUA

Ancient People of the Flagstaff Region

by Peter J. Pilles, Jr.

Wupatki National Monument. Left to right, visitor center, ruins and amphitheater, ball court. Photo by Paul Logsdon, 1986.

The Early Sinagua: A.D. 675–1064

THE EARLIEST EVIDENCE of the Sinagua dates to about A.D. 675. While the exact origins of these south-western people still remain cloudy, it appears likely that they gradually moved into the San Francisco Peaks region from the southeast, following the forested zone between the Little Colorado River and the Mogollon Rim. Their settlements consisted of pithouse villages, each of which was probably occupied by related families. The settlements are generally situated in areas that today are transitional between the ponderosa pine and piñon-juniper zones. By locating themselves in these transition areas, the Sinagua were able to make use of the wild plant and animal resources of both environmental zones. In addition to these natural resources, cultivated crops were also an important part of their diet, and villages were located close to the best farming soils. On the whole, most soils in the San Francisco Peaks region are poor for farming, but fertile, loamy soils are found in the large basins, locally known as "parks," along the flanks of the Peaks and Anderson Mesa. On the edges of these parks we find the early Sinagua villages.

At a few sites, extremely large pithouses are found; these are thought to be "community rooms," where people from different villages came together at various times of the year to conduct ceremonial and social functions. The recognition of such specialized sites is important, for it suggests that Sinagua social organization extended beyond the single family unit. In fact, rather than being simple, isolated, mountain folk, as some authors have suggested, it appears that the Sinagua were more highly organized and culturally complex than previously thought. Pottery sherds indicate that in addition to this regional interaction, the Sinagua had relationships with the Hohokam to the south in the Salt River Valley and with the Kayenta Anasazi to the north.

Rock-terraced fields, Pollack site, Anderson Mesa. Illustration by Marvin Marcroft.

The population at this early time was fairly small, but by A.D. 900, it had increased and was centered along the eastern flank of the San Francisco Peaks. This distribution may have been due to a climatic change to warmer and drier conditions. With this change, many of the Sinagua may have moved to the Peaks vicinity, where springs and snow provided perennial water. In addition, clouds generated by the Peaks would have provided more rainfall in that area than elsewhere in the Sinagua region.

By this time, pithouse architecture had become more varied. Stones or timber were sometimes used to line pithouse walls, and shallow structures outlined with large rocks and walled with brush appeared. In addition to the large community rooms, ball courts also occur at a few of the community room sites. Their presence indicates not only increased relationships with other cultures but also a willingness to accept and experiment with new customs.

The Sinagua developed new farming techniques to utilize a wider range of soil types. In addition to planting in the alluvial parks, the people had fields at the mouths of washes where they entered the parks, and they constructed terraces to catch water and soil run-off at higher elevations along the flanks of the Peaks. The Sinagua built small fieldhouses of stone, precursors of the pueblos that characterize their later history. These fieldhouses were constructed near the terraces for use during the spring and summer farming seasons. By planting in a variety of situations, they were able to maximize their chances of obtaining a bountiful harvest, whatever the weather conditions. Besides the purposeful planting of crops, the Sinagua likely encouraged a variety of natural plants to grow in their fields. Analysis of pollen from prehistoric sites suggests that beeweed, amaranths, grasses, wild buckwheat, goosefoot, pigweed, mustard, and wild onion were useful economic plants.

Pithouse, A.D. 900–1064. Illustration by Marvin Marcroft.

Sunset Crater. Photo by Paul Logsdon, 1986.

Sunset Crater's History

For many years, archaeologists have known that people lived in the area when the volcano that formed Sunset Crater erupted. A major focus of archaeological work in the 1930s was to investigate the effects of the eruption on prehistoric cultural developments. The theory has been that the crater erupted in the fall of 1064 and the spring of 1066, spreading a blanket of cinders over an 800-square-mile area. Within this region, disintegrating cinders added nutrients to the soil and also acted as a mulch that retarded moisture evaporation. Thus a vast area suitable for agriculture was created and, according to the traditional interpretation, news of this new farmland spread far and wide, precipitating a prehistoric land rush. Archaeologists theorized that people from six different culture areas migrated to the Flagstaff vicinity to take advantage of these new farmlands, and that the resultant interaction between these migrants and the local Sinagua dramatically changed the course of cultural development in the area. A great population increase, new pottery styles, architectural forms, burial practices, jewelry, religious systems, and many other aspects of Sinagua culture after 1066 have been attributed to this supposed blending of cultures.

However, a different picture is emerging, based on advances in archaeological theories of cultural change, new archaeological data, re-examination of old data, and new geological information. It now appears that the eruptions of Sunset Crater continued for a much longer period than previously believed, with cinder eruptions taking place episodically between 1064 and 1250. This long-term cycle, typical of most volcanoes, began about September of 1064, when a ten-mile-long fissure developed five miles southeast of what was to become the crater. This phenomenon was accompanied by a five-mile-long flow of lava to the east and deep accumulations of black cinders over a twelve-by-fifteen-mile-wide area. Another eruption between the growing seasons of 1066 and 1067 may have occurred, although this is doubted by some authorities. Within a few decades, the first stage of the Sunset Crater cinder cone was formed. During the next thirty years or so, the volcano produced more than half a billion tons of

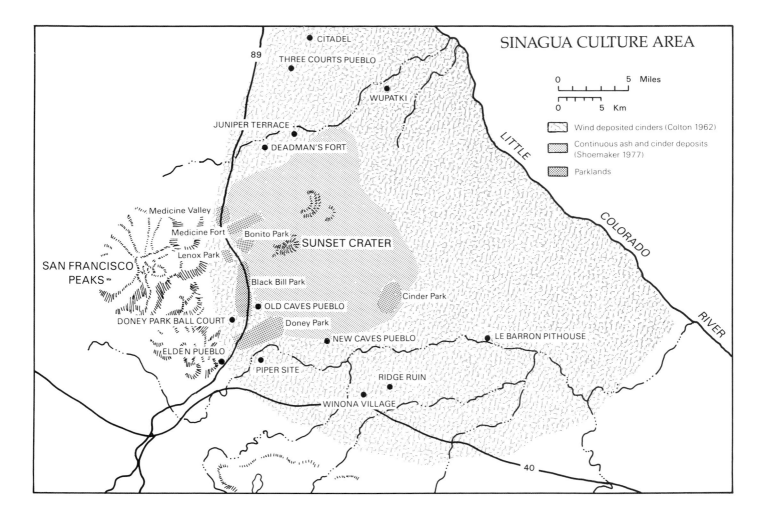

SINAGUA CULTURE AREA

Wind deposited cinders (Colton 1962)

Continuous ash and cinder deposits (Shoemaker 1977)

Parklands

cinders, which the winds carried to blanket the 800-square-mile area. Although the winds blew primarily to the northeast, cinders from Sunset Crater have been identified at Meteor Crater, Cameron, and even as far away as Kansas. In 1150, the Kana-a Flow oozed from the northeast side of the cone to fill Kana-a Wash with molten lava as more cinders were blown out. Between 1180 and 1200, a number of fumaroles developed along a fissure that ran southeast from Sunset Crater, forming Gyp Crater and depositing red cinders over the area. In 1220, the Bonito Flow broke forth from the west side of the crater, and more cinders were produced, repairing this breach. A mound of cinders on top of the Bonito Flow may be either a part of the breached cone or a small satellite crater; it has been named Yaponcha, after the Hopi wind god associated with the cinder cone area.

Yaponcha was disturbed by later lava movement that also squeezed up cracks on the edges of the Bonito Flow. A lava tube drained onto the Kana-a Flow somewhat later, and finally, in 1250, the 200-year sequence of volcanism ended with the deposition of red cinders along the rim of the cone. In 1885, their rosy hue prompted Major John Wesley Powell to name the crater "Sunset," because it appears to be eternally illuminated by the rays of the setting sun.

Effects of the Eruption: Old and New Ideas

The importance of the cinders as a fertilizing and mulching medium has been overrated. Although cinders can add many nutrients to the soil, this process usually takes hundreds or thousands of years—a time frame that would extend long after the Sinagua had disappeared. Even today, pine trees growing in the cinder fields are stunted and have many large, right-angled branches, rather than the tall, straight growth of normal ponderosa pines. These characteristics indicate that the trees are growing under stress rather than with the benefit of the postulated fertile conditions.

The evidence for the major migration to the area is based upon the occurrences of certain artifacts, architecture, and burials thought to be distinctive for particular cultural groups. Yet these are all isolated occurrences at many different sites. No complete *assemblage* of architecture and artifacts characterizing a different cultural group has been found. Many of the supposed immigrant artifacts are jewelry or pottery that can be more readily explained as trade items. Many of the architectural traits supposedly brought in by the immigrants actually have pre-eruption antecedents. The "amphitheater" at Wupatki, for example,

5

has been cited as a Chaco Anasazi Great Kiva. In fact, it is most likely a community room, a feature found at major Sinagua sites from their earliest beginnings. Similarly, the use of masonry architecture, supposedly introduced by the Cohonina or Anasazi, can also be found in sites predating the initial eruption. The new artifact types, architecture, and burial practices may actually indicate increasing participation of the Sinagua in regional exchange systems and, as noted earlier, an open-minded attitude towards trying new concepts, rather than the physical presence of people from different cultures.

The evidence for the supposed population increase may actually reflect a change in the farming technology employed by the Sinagua as they adjusted to a different environment. Following 1064, people began to move to lower elevations in the piñon-juniper zone. In most of this zone, soils are shallow and occur in a few broad wash bottoms and in small pockets of soil that have formed in the limestone bedrock. In order to utilize the soil pockets, fieldhouses were constructed, and each family would likely have several such pockets to tend during the summer farming months. After several seasons, the crops would sap the nutrients in the soil pockets, and the Sinagua farmers would move to new farm plots and build new fieldhouses.

With this scenario, it would not take long for hundreds of fieldhouses to be constructed, accounting for the supposed increase in population. Thus, although the numbers of *sites* increased, this phenomenon may not represent increase in the number of *people*. The increase in sites is due to larger numbers of seasonally occupied fieldhouses, not habitation sites where people lived for most of the year.

Some have doubted this theory, questioning whether the Sinagua could actually have overfarmed so heavily. They also suggest that soil nutrients would have been replenished after a few seasons if the earth lay fallow. However, soils in the Flagstaff area are very susceptible to nutrient depletion. In particular, corn extracts great amounts of nitrogen from the soil. An indication of how permanently soils can be depleted of nutrients is shown by chemical tests on soils from a prehistoric field southeast of Wupatki National Monument. When compared to adjacent soils that had not been farmed, they were found to be still significantly depleted—over 700 years later!

Finally, if the cinder fall was as important as previously believed, one would expect a higher site density within the cinder zone than outside of it. Yet archaeological surveys find site densities outside the cinder fall to be just as high as within the cinder zone.

Much of the change in Sinagua settlement and land use after 1064 can be explained by a major environmental change. Tree-ring and pollen studies show the period between 1050 and 1150 was one of above-average rainfall accompanied by a warming trend. Much of this increase was caused by summer rains, rather than winter snows, a factor that would greatly benefit crops during the dry summer growing season.

Thus, the large-scale population shift that characterizes the post-1064 period is not related to the cinder fields, but is caused by people moving to the lower elevations that could be successfully farmed because of increased moisture. The fact that much of this area falls within the limits of Sunset Crater's ash fall is only coincidental. The one area that may have benefited from the cinder-mulching effect is the Wupatki Basin. There, the effect of moisture-retaining cinders, combined with increased precipitation, may have offset the extremely dry conditions of the Little Colorado River Valley and allowed productive farming.

Fieldhouse east of Strawberry Crater. Photo by Peter Pilles, 1983.

Bonito Lava Flow and Sunset Crater. Photo by George Huey, 1986.

After Sunset Crater's Eruption

Just as Sinagua pithouse and pueblo villages spread throughout the piñon-juniper zone, so did Sinagua culture grow and expand between 1064 and 1150. Pithouse styles show similarities with earlier forms, but many new styles were tried until stone-lined pithouses with roof entry became the most common form. Many houses after 1100 are smaller than earlier ones, suggesting changes in family composition and size. Kivas also became more standardized; the structures were underground and masonry-lined, with a raised bench across one end.

The continued presence of large, masonry-lined, underground community rooms, which are also found in earlier times, suggests social relationships outside of the individual village. The community rooms occasionally have a rectangular entryway on one side. Some of the community room sites are also associated with ball courts, and there are indications that certain villages began to have greater importance in regional affairs and trade activities.

Formal cemeteries and burial mounds are recognizable, and they hint at more complex religious development. The different burial types—cremations, extended burials, and flexed burials—suggest that several belief systems were held at this time. In addition, some cemeteries are formally arranged according to the different burial types. In one area cremations are found, while extended burials are found in the other part of the cemetery. The presence of cremations has traditionally been interpreted as proof of a Hohokam population that cremated its dead; however, recent studies of the skeletal remains and burial offerings suggest that the burials are unlike Hohokam and are simply the remains of a Sinagua population that cremated its dead.

The Elden Phase

Between about 1150 and 1250, Sinagua culture blossomed and reached its greatest technological and organizational heights. This period is known as the Elden Phase and is named after Elden Pueblo, which is located at the northern edge of present-day Flagstaff and is one of the largest and most famous sites of this period. The main occupation of most other well-known sites in the area, such as Wupatki, Walnut Canyon, Ridge Ruin, and New Caves, dates to this phase. Although the population was concentrated into fewer but larger sites, all portions of the Flagstaff region were occupied from the San Francisco Peaks to East Clear Creek and from the Wupatki area to the forest zone along the Mogollon Rim.

Over the years, the cliff dwellings and large pueblos of this phase have attracted the most attention, while the range of architecture of this period has been overlooked.

Life at Elden Pueblo. Illustration by Brian Donahue.

Textbooks and museum displays usually state that pithouses were replaced by pueblos at this time, paralleling architectural evolution elsewhere in the Southwest after A.D. 1100. However, we now know that pithouses continued beyond 1100 and, in fact, that they occur throughout the entire cultural sequence in most of the Southwest. The Sinagua pithouses of the time are usually square or rectangular and lined with masonry. Kivas and community rooms are the same as those found earlier.

As village sizes increased, more sophisticated organization was needed to integrate and oversee the activities of the population as well as its relationships with outside groups. The existence of complex and highly developed organizational systems is indicated by site sizes, village plans, regular spacing between villages, differential treatment of the dead, and unique artifact forms. A hierarchy of settlement types illustrates these different levels of importance in the Sinagua system. The most important of these site types consists of a small number of pueblos that have highly distinctive characteristics. These sites, which might be called "chief" villages, include Wupatki, Ridge Ruin, Juniper Terrace, and, from a somewhat earlier time, Three Courts Pueblo and Winona Village. All lie along likely prehistoric trade routes, are located on hilltops, have a community room as well as inner and outer courtyards delineated by stone walls, and are associated with ball courts. Such sites have a greater than average quantity of tradeware pottery and exotic artifacts, and they were likely inhabited by the religious, social, and political leaders of the day.

Further evidence of social stratification and the existence of social hierarchies is found in the burials of this period, most notably the "Magician's Burial" at Ridge Ruin.

Ridge Ruin, among the trees, and two craterlike ball courts. Photo by Peter Pilles, 1978.

The Magician was buried with over 600 objects, including dozens of pottery vessels, hundreds of projectile points, painted baskets, quantities of mineral pigment, shell and stone jewelry, miniature bows and arrows, a beaded cap, shell tinklers, a large nose plug, a staff, mosaic-encrusted shell jewelry and basketry, and a unique series of wooden wands. These were carved and painted into the forms of deer or antelope hoofs, human hands, and serrated shapes; and three of each of these forms were buried with the Magician. Hopis who have viewed this amazing assemblage recognize the ceremonial use of the items and have identified the Magician as a very important person in the *Motswimi*, or Warrior, Society. Not only does the Magician's Burial suggest a Sinagua ancestry for the Hopi, but most importantly it demonstrates the existence of religious societies by the thirteenth century. The presence of religious societies signals a significant level of social organization and village interaction that is very important for understanding Sinagua culture.

Other examples of rank and status among the Sinagua have been found in high-status burials at other sites, such as Elden Pueblo. Certain unique artifacts accompanying these burials seem to have been symbols by which the individual's authority could be recognized by other people. These include nose plugs, carved or painted bone hairpins, staffs with elaborate knobs or carvings at the top, wands tipped with painted sea shells, conch-shell trumpets, and unique pottery vessels. Today, similar items are used by the high priests of Hopi societies as symbols of their status and responsibility. In addition, some petroglyphs portray these items being held or worn by people in obvious positions of importance.

The Beginning of the End: A.D. 1250–1300

The dynamic days of the Elden Phase came to an end in the latter part of the thirteenth century, during a time when the climate became cooler and drier, and precipitation shifted to a winter or early spring pattern. It appears that the extensive territory occupied during the Elden Phase was abandoned, and the population concentrated at a few locations in the Mt. Elden, Doney Park, Anderson Mesa, Wupatki, and Ridge Ruin areas. Proximity to a reliable water source apparently was an important consideration, for most of these sites are located close to springs.

A possible indication of difficult times may be "forts," found in earlier times as well as during this period. They were built atop hills and prominences on high cinder cones and at the ends of promontories extending into steep-walled canyons. Some forts have walls, strategically placed to restrict access, or loopholes directed to avenues of approach. The forts are usually interpreted as places of refuge during times of hostilities. However, no evidence of warfare has been found. Furthermore, if such friction existed, an accompanying cessation of trade would be expected. Yet the quantity of tradeware pottery found at forts is the same as that at other sites, indicating trade did

Petroglyph of a man with cane and free-form design of simple hooks. Photo by David Noble, 1986.

not stop during this time. The defensive posture of such sites may reflect a general wariness, akin to our bomb-shelter craze during the 1950s. Some have suggested that rather than being used for defense or warfare-related functions, the forts served as communal storehouses for food and other commodities, the residences of elite families or individuals, or as astronomical observatories.

However, archaeologists are now studying another interpretation, one more closely related to sociological development. Through time, with the growth of social hierarchies and perhaps competition in trade markets, a sense of community came about. Territorial boundaries would have been established to provide a dependable resource area to support the community and to reaffirm separation from surrounding communities. According to this interpretation, the forts may have defined and marked the boundaries of specific communities and could have been way stations for those entering the territory of another group.

Shell jewelry from Chavez Pass. Photo by Peter Pilles.

The End of the Sinagua Tradition: A.D. 1300–1400

By 1300, only Old Caves Pueblo remained occupied in the traditional Sinagua heartland east of the San Francisco Peaks. That site has the characteristics of the so-called chief villages, including a hilltop location and a community room, as well as a ball court that was only recently discovered. Most of the Sinagua population either abandoned the region completely or moved to other areas such as Wupatki or Anderson Mesa. On Anderson Mesa, six large pueblos at Kinnikinick, Grapevine, the Pollock Site, and Nuvakwewtaqa constitute the last stage of the Sinagua. At these sites, we can see the Sinagua tradition merging into that of the Hopi.

According to our current theories, the largest and most important of these six great pueblo towns were the three pueblos of Nuvakwewtaqa in Chavez Pass. Located in a natural corridor between northern and central Arizona, this location is thought to be a dominant node in a trade route between these areas. In the sixteenth century, Spanish explorers were told by the Hopi that the pass was on a very old trail that ran from the Hopi Mesas to the Homolovi ruins near Winslow, to Chavez Pass, to Stoneman Lake, and into the Verde Valley. In fact, evidence of trade—such as turquoise, mineral pigments, shell jewelry, obsidian, pottery, and even a copper bell from Mexico—is abundant at Nuvakwewtaqa. Relationships with settlements in the Verde Valley are suggested by the fact that the tradeware pottery found at 1300–1400 period sites in the Verde Valley are those types found so conspicuously at Nuvakwewtaqa.

It is also significant that Nuvakwewtaqa has those features by which the chief villages can be identified as well as other constructions such as reservoirs, stairways to a nearby spring, a massive retaining wall, smaller community rooms, extensive petroglyphs, and elaborate terraced fields. Archaeologists disagree about the identification of the ball court; however, the presence of the other chief village characteristics and ball courts at other late sites, such as Old Caves, suggests that the Nuvakwewtaqa feature served this function.

Another feature common to the Anderson Mesa pueblos is that they are surrounded by large numbers of rock-outlined field sites. Mapping and testing of these fields indicates trash was intentionally added to the soil, probably as fertilizer, and that the people captured and distributed soil and water run-off across the field system.

Such features take much time to construct and maintain, and considerable effort evidently went into growing food for the population. However, it has recently been suggested that these farming efforts were inadequate to support the population and that food may have been the commodity the Verde Valley pueblos traded to their Anderson Mesa relatives.

After 1400, the great pueblos were deserted, and the Sinagua can no longer be recognized as a distinct cultural group. Archaeological evidence tends to support Hopi traditions about the site and suggests the people moved to the Homolovi sites before continuing to the Hopi Mesas, where their descendants live today. Many lines of evidence at Nuvakwewtaqa indicate a Hopi relationship. Petroglyphs around the ruins portray masked beings that may be kachinas or other types of masked personages. Various figures of Hopi legend and folklore—such as Pöqangwhoya, one of the War Twins; Kokopelli, the hump-backed flute player; and the Shalako kachina—have been found portrayed on pottery at the site. In addition, Hopi traditions recount a number of clans that passed through Chavez Pass and specifically recognize Nuvakwewtaqa as an ancestral home of the Water, Sun Forehead, and Side Corn clans.

Further ties of the Hopi to the prehistoric Sinagua are indicated by the ceremonial, religious, and ancestral importance they place upon various locations in the prehistoric Sinagua region. Several ruins, such as Wupatki, Nuvakwewtaqa, and Elden Pueblo, known to the Hopi as Pasiwvi, are specifically identified as ancestral villages. Areas throughout the Sinagua region, such as Walnut Canyon, Canyon Padre, Meteor Crater, and various places around the San Francisco Peaks, are traditional eagle-collecting areas, marked by a series of shrines. The Sunset Crater area is the home of Yaponcha, god of the winds. Most significantly, the San Francisco Peaks themselves are the home of most of the kachinas and a major focus of Hopi religious activities. This religious importance was likely shared by the prehistoric Sinagua.

Hopi Water Clan petroglyph at Nuvakwewtaqa. Photo by Peter Pilles, 1976.

This article has briefly sketched old and new theories about the prehistoric people who inhabited the area around the San Francisco Peaks. While the major outline of their history has been fairly well established, the important details are far from being understood, and much additional work is needed before the complete story of the Sinagua is known. Changing concepts of cultural development, environmental change, and general anthropological theory provide new frameworks with which to examine old and new data. While archaeologists often argue about the interpretations, all agree that the Sinagua played an important role in the history and development of north-central Arizona. Their accomplishments over eight centuries have earned the respect of archaeologists and the admiration of all who view their remains today.

Peter J. Pilles, Jr., is the forest archaeologist at Coconino National Forest in Flagstaff, Arizona.

Box Canyon Ruin in 1926. Courtesy, Milwaukee Public Museum.

WUPATKI
NATIONAL MONUMENT
Exploring into Prehistory

by Bruce A. Anderson

STANDING IN THE CITADEL RUIN, today's traveler gazes over black basalt mesas topped with red sandstone ruins and tries to picture the prehistoric world of 700 years ago. Squinting and using his imagination, he can envision complete rooms of fine masonry, covered with roofs of wood and clay. Families weed the cornfields on Antelope Prairie to the east, while a hunting party in search of deer moves southwest to the San Francisco Peaks.

The blazing heat of mid-July interrupts these visions of the past. A lizard seeks shade under a rock ledge. The traveler pulls a frosty soft drink from a cooler in his air-conditioned car and drives on to the nearest trading post for food staples and other conveniences. But as he departs, questions linger in his mind.

Where did the people who once lived in these broken-down pueblos find water in this harsh, arid land? How did they eke out a living from this barren soil? How did they cope with the vast distances of the desert Southwest, with no means of transportation other than their feet?

These questions are only part of Wupatki National Monument's complex archaeological puzzle. This alluring region of northern Arizona still holds many perplexing enigmas which the National Park Service is attempting to answer through the extensive, seven-year Wupatki Archaeological Inventory Survey Project.

The Archaeological Survey

In 1973, I worked on the initial programming for an archaeological inventory survey for Wupatki National Monument. Little did I know that eight years later I would be directing the project. In the early 1970s, estimates put the number of archaeological sites within the boundaries of Wupatki at about eight hundred. Now that most of the monument's 35,254 acres have been surveyed and inventoried, projections set the number at a minimum of 2,700 sites. However, there was a dearth of information on the variation of sites, the cultures involved, and the range of environmental conditions—all factors that help to determine the density of archaeologial sites.

I began the first summer of fieldwork for the survey in 1981, accompanied by four assistants. We soon found the summer weather conditions at Wupatki to be nearly unbearable, especially when temperatures

Bruce Anderson, left, and crew member on survey on Antelope Prairie, 1982. Courtesy, National Park Service.

rose above 110 degrees—without a shade tree in sight. Our work was primarily on black cinders and basalt slopes that absorbed and radiated the sun's heat. The latter half of the summer brought dangerous thunderstorms during which individuals on the survey crews stood like lightning rods on the flat, barren desert.

The actual survey process was rigorous and demanding. On our initial pass the surveyors walked transects through a section of land (one square mile) with each person spaced no more than ten meters from the next. As crew members found archaeological features, they stuck pin flags in the ground and then plotted them on a large-scale map.

Once this phase was completed, we were ready to return to the section and begin the recording process. We assigned numbers to features or groups of features that represented a single site unit. On a six-page form describing each site and its exact geographic location, we recorded the environmental conditions and the artifacts present. On the form we could make recommendations for protection and/or further work needed at the site.

The crew also located each site on aerial photographs and topographic maps and drew detailed plan maps. We photographed all features at the site and collected artifacts for further study. The entire process of surveying one section took three to four weeks.

(In subsequent field seasons, I utilized two to three survey crews to assist in the work.)

Most of the prehistoric sites surveyed at Wupatki show a mixing of cultures: Kayenta Anasazi, Winslow Anasazi, Sinagua, Prescott, and Cohonina. The names of these cultures have been assigned by archaeologists. *Anasazi* is a Navajo word that can be roughly translated as "Ancient Ones," while *Kayenta* and *Winslow* refer to the geographic areas of the cultures. *Sinagua* is taken from the Spanish words meaning "without water." *Prescott* also refers to the location of the cultural group of that name. *Cohonina* comes from a Hopi word for the people who lived in the Grand Canyon area. Evidence of these cultures comes primarily from distinctive architecture and definitive pottery types.

After several years of surveying, we have found site patterns that indicate settlement for most advantageous land use. The western half of the monument, Antelope Prairie, is higher in elevation and appears to have been more densely populated, probably because of more precipitation and better soils in that area. In

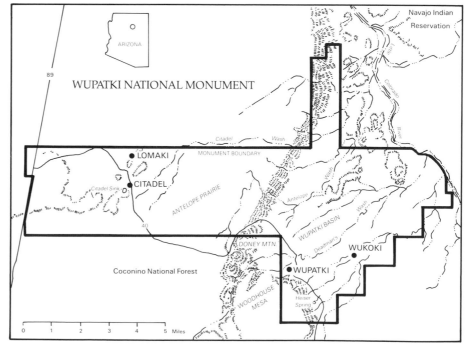

this region, we found the bulk of Wupatki's agricultural features. Rock piles in fields may have been boundary markers. Stones were aligned to serve as field borders and may also have protected crops from high spring winds as well as acting as retainers to slow run-off. Check dams in small drainages controlled water flow, and larger dams in natural catchments helped store water. Rock terraces on slopes provided flat, fertile farm plots. Hundreds of fieldhouses, which were normally single-room structures, provided shelter from the elements for those tending crops.

Although the survey located pueblo dwellings scattered throughout the monument, the largest pueblos, containing at least five rooms, were below Antelope Prairie

along major drainages. Evidence shows that these water courses were not permanent water sources at the time, but they may have provided intermittent supply. Natural rock shelters along canyon walls were often used as temporary campsites. We found rock enclosures and rock art—petroglyphs—in many.

In our survey we dated most archaeological remains by ceramic types found on the surface of the ground. Only a few tree-ring dates can be obtained in this area.

Most historic and recent Navajo occupation, indicated by hogans, corrals, and sweat lodges, has been in the eastern half of the monument. Close proximity to the Little Colorado River may account for the Navajos' preference for this area.

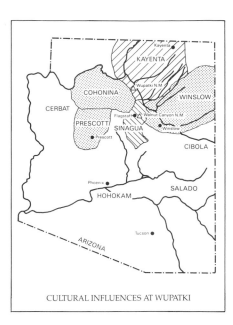

CULTURAL INFLUENCES AT WUPATKI

Circular fieldhouse, pueblo in background, 1982. Courtesy, National Park Service.

The Citadel. Photo by George Huey, 1986.

Main ruin at Wupatki. Photo by George Huey, 1986.

Lomaki Ruin. Photo by George Huey, 1986.

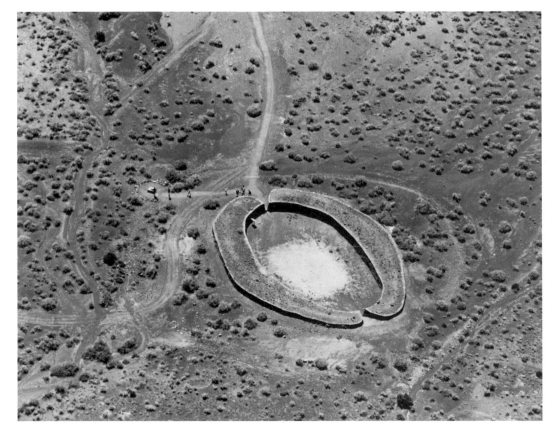

Ball court at Wupatki. Photo by Paul Logsdon, 1986.

Clovis point. Photo by Bill Crowder.

Early Cultures

The earliest remains from Wupatki are two spearpoints, one a Clovis point approximately 11,000 years old and the other an Agate Basin point fragment dating from 8,000 years ago. A few other projectile points can be attributed to Archaic people, who were nomadic hunters and gatherers who utilized the area until about A.D. 500. These early groups made use of gravel terraces along the Little Colorado River formed during the Pleistocene epoch. They are also associated with the "Tolchaco Focus," the name given by early archaeologists to the numerous lithic workshop areas found atop the terraces. Here the prehistoric people selected stones appropriate for tool manufacture. Later groups also used these lithic sites to gather stone materials for projectile points and other tools. We have found points composed of the same materials scattered throughout the monument.

One period of Wupatki's cultural development extends from about A.D. 500 until the major eruptions of Sunset Crater in 1064–66. This time is reflected in about a dozen sites at which the cinder and ash cover has eroded away. The earlier portion of this period reveals the beginnings of horticulture and small pithouse villages, as well as community interaction which is evidenced by widespread pottery types. Later remains indicate an increased dependence on domesticated crops over hunting and gathering as well as movement toward building aboveground masonry structures. Pottery types tend to be localized, indicating that the individual village was the primary social unit. Trade was less prevalent than in later periods.

After Sunset Crater's Eruption

Early archaeologists working in the region suggested that following the eruptions a massive influx of people moved into the Flagstaff area—a sort of prehistoric land rush—primarily because of beneficial effects of the soil's moisture retention caused by the extensive cinder cover. However, another possible reason for the population increase is that changes in weather patterns about the time of the major eruptions brought more precipitation. This phenomenon may better explain the increased usage of the Wupatki area as well as pan-Southwest movements of prehistoric people. We may never know how much the usage of the Wupatki region increased after the eruption because pre-eruption sites are now buried beneath cinders and lava flows.

By the mid-1100s, the moister climate changed to semi-arid conditions, and farming became more difficult. By about A.D. 1225, the Wupatki area was abandoned. The last tree-ring cutting date for Wupatki Pueblo is A.D. 1212, and we have no evidence to indicate other occupations until historic times.

Most of our knowledge about this period is based on the excavations of Wupatki and Nalakihu pueblos in the 1930s. At Wupatki, archaeologists found numerous pieces of turquoise and shell jewelry; copper bells; human and parrot burials; and extensive textiles, such as woven baskets, sashes, and cotton fibers. The presence of marine shells and of turquoise, copper, and parrots indicates far-reaching trade. At Nalakihu archaeologists discovered small clay ovens, a cremation, more shells and parrots, and a high percentage of Prescott ceramics, suggesting trade links to the south. Even the ball court at Wupatki was an idea that originated in Mexico and Central America.

Today, several of the largest and most significant ancient pueblos at Wupatki are open to the public. The Park Service at Wupatki National Monument provides interpretive information for Wupatki Pueblo, located immediately behind the visitor center. Nalakihu, the Citadel, and Lomaki can be reached along the main monument road, while Wukoki requires a short side trip on a paved road.

Historic Use

By about A.D. 1825, the Navajo were using Wupatki in the vicinity of Black Point, north of Crack-In-Rock Pueblo. There is no evidence of earlier Navajo use, but Hopis may have traveled through the area prior to this time. Both the Navajos and Hopis consider parts of Wupatki to be sacred

and have built shrines in those locations. A few early Hopi sites have been identified by ceramics found during the survey, but no definite dates exist for these sites. Later in the 1800s and up to the present, Navajos settled primarily in the Little Colorado River Basin, particularly in the Black Falls area.

In the late 1800s and early 1900s, two trading posts operated in the area. Across the river at Tolchaco was a mission school, and the CO Bar Ranch was established to the north while Ben Doney was mining near Doney Mountain. These activities reflect Anglo settlement prior to the creation of Wupatki National Monument in 1924.

The Survey Record

The Wupatki Archaeological Inventory Survey Project has required an immense amount of time and effort, but it has brought rewards, such as the Clovis point, a complete Pueblo III basket recovered from an earth crack, two whole ceramic vessels, and a revolver dated about 1873.

A small corrugated vessel from a cache near the Citadel. Courtesy, National Park Service.

Such intriguing discoveries have made the project worthwile. However, most of the finds have been fragmentary ceramics and pieces of stone tools or remnants of their manufacture, which help to date periods of site occupations. In areas of high visitation, tourists' and pothunters' collection of potsherds and other artifacts in earlier years has totally eliminated the records, making it impossible to date these sites.

One of the primary goals of the survey has been to provide the National Park Service and the professional archaeological community with current research on Wupatki. However, another equally important goal has been to provide interpretive information for public programs. Our purpose is achieved if, when the traveler stands atop Citadel Ruin, he has a clearer understanding of the prehistoric peoples who lived there and is able to sense the difficulties of surviving in this harsh desert environment.

Bruce Anderson is an archaeologist with the National Park Service at Wupatki National Monument.

Pueblo III basket recovered by the survey. Photo by Bill Crowder.

Textile patterns as petroglyphs, North Mesa. The over-all "limitless" design of the lower petroglyph is typical of Sinagua weaving. The smaller pattern above with a central focus was more typical of contemporary Anasazi textiles. Photo by David Noble, 1986.

Rock Art at Wupatki

Pots, Textiles, Glyphs

by Polly Schaafsma

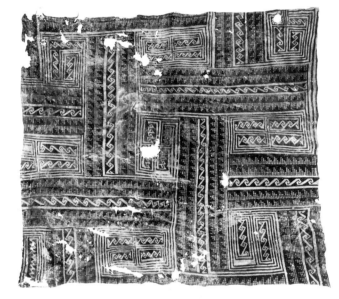

THROUGHOUT THE BROAD VISTAS of the Painted Desert and the volcanic plateaus near Wupatki National Monument are black-faced basalt escarpments and light red sandstone cliffs and boulders that bear man-made images from southwestern prehistory. The petroglyphs include animals, human figures, and a variety of geometric patterns. The recent archaeological inventory survey of Wupatki located sixty-nine rock-art sites. Some are found near the ruins once inhabited by people who made the rock art, while others are located at considerable distances from former dwellings.

Rock art has been made in the Southwest for a wide variety of reasons. The subject matter is often religious and may have been executed in connection with ritual functions. Some rock art is viewed by the modern Pueblos as a record or validation of the historic/mythic past. Within recent times the use of rock art to mark social and political boundaries is well documented.

In the Wupatki area, a handful of recent rock-art figures were made historically by Hopis. Most are clan symbols very similar to those carved at the well-known Hopi shrine on the Salt Trail at Willow Springs some forty miles to the north of Wupatki. Among the petroglyphs at a site just outside the eastern boundary of the monument, the crane (or crow?), corn, and kachina clans are represented. This site is fairly close to a trail, described by Dr. Harold Sellers Colton, that runs between the Hopi mesas and the San Francisco

Above right:
Sinagua textile from Hidden House, Arizona, A.D. 1100–1300. The basic pattern painted on this piece of cloth also occurs in Sinagua petroglyphs and ceramic decoration. Photo by E. B. Sayles. Courtesy, Arizona State Museum.

Above left:
Black-on-white pottery from Wupatki Ruin. The limitless pattern on the large bowl resembles textile and petroglyph patterns from the region. Photo by David Noble, 1986.

Flute players, a hunter with bow and arrow, a mountain lion, deer, a variety of other animals, tracks, a spiral, and a complex outlined cross comprise this group of early Pueblo petroglyphs. Photo by David Noble, 1986.

Peaks. Possibly the clan symbols were pecked there by Hopis to document their participation in ritual trips to the mountains.

The prehistoric petroglyphs at Wupatki display an array of animals including stylized mountain lions, distinguished by tails that curve over their backs; some equivocal antelope pursued by a hunter with bow and arrow; a few possible mountain sheep, deer, and lizards; a few birds; various insects; and a number of unidentifiable creatures, some of which exceed the naturalistic realm. Also depicted are large human footprints or bear tracks. The human beings and/or anthropomorphic supernaturals are engaged in a variety of lively activities such as hunting, sexual intercourse, giving birth, and playing flutes. Scenes with figures interacting as a group seem to depict either mythical or ceremonial events. Important figures are distinguished by hair-bobs or long earrings, and they carry hooked staffs.

Large spirals are a noteworthy component of Wupatki rock art. Various interpretations have been suggested for this basic element: it may symbolize water or wind, or have an association with the sun, especially if the rock art is positioned so that it interacts with a beam or shaft of light. To modern Hopis and Zunis the spiral represents migrations. The last interpretation could easily apply to one complex of large spirals in which human figures (and other life forms?) are shown on extended lines or "paths" leading into the spirals.

Other abstract motifs include outlined crosses and interlocking rectilinear scrolls shown in combination with barbed lines. The latter resemble pottery designs. There are also complicated patterns and decorative bands similar to those seen in prehistoric textile fragments. Finally, less formalized meanders appear, sometimes combined with simple spirals. The textile- and pottery-like

designs, which are particularly outstanding in Sinagua rock art, are important components of these petroglyphs, not only because of their striking aesthetic qualities but also because of their archaeological significance. Comparing rock-art patterns with decorations on prehistoric textile fragments and pottery is one means of dating the petroglyphs, and it also provides information on the complex cultural affiliations in the Sinagua region.

The Wupatki petroglyph textile patterns are of exceptional quality and complexity. Some are framed as if a blanket were represented, and others are unbounded. The following discussion is based on Kate Peck Kent's analysis of the remains of prehistoric textiles, which have been preserved throughout the Southwest at archaeological sites in dry caves and rock shelters.

Of the six major textile petroglyph designs illustrated here, five depict typical late prehistoric weavings which were made after A.D. 1000 on wide looms introduced into the northern Southwest from southern Arizona. The wide looms contributed to a new handling of space in woven patterns and to the development of new designs. The overall designs of the petroglyph textile patterns can basically be seen as oblique bands offset around interlocking motifs.

Four of the petroglyphs depict an overall limitless pattern lacking a central motif, a design style typical of Sinagua weaving. The largest of these petroglyphs of endless Sinagua-like patterns is pecked on basalt at the edge of North Mesa. It is reminiscent of a slightly more complex pattern found on a brocaded cotton fragment from further south in Sinagua territory near Camp Verde, below the Mogollon Rim. A common element in Sinagua design, the smooth-edged triangle tooth pattern, arranged in oblique opposing rows, is found in both this petroglyph and the textile fragment. This element may have originated to the south, as it is common in the Salado region. The interlocking hooked triangles in the weaving are simplified in the petroglyph. The overall pattern is closely related to Hohokam textile designs.

Bizarre lizard forms and geometric designs. The band of interlocking hooks is a common Sinagua-Salado motif. The complex rectilinear scrolls and barbed lines echo pottery designs. Photo by David Noble, 1986.

Pottery motifs as petroglyphs. These interlocking rectilinear scrolls and barbed lines resemble local Pueblo II ceramic designs (A.D. 1070–1120). Photo by David Noble, 1986.

In contrast, the smaller textile design pecked above the petroglyph just discussed has a central focus. The pattern is more typical of late Pueblo III (A.D. 1200–1300) textiles represented in Anasazi rock art and of designs painted on Anasazi cotton cloth. The Wupatki petroglyphs are notably lacking, however, in the terraced triangular element, an ancient and favorite Anasazi motif, almost ubiquitous in both textile and ceramic designs.

A rather anomalous petroglyph textile is divided by two crossed bands containing negative diamond or rectangular elements with central dots. Attached to these bands are simple hooks used as separate elements. This finite overall pattern is unusual and so is the particular combination of details. Negative rectangles are a feature of Pueblo III and IV Anasazi tie-dye patterns on cotton cloth, while the simple hook is frequently used in Hohokam textiles.

The plain hook lacking a triangular base is also present in a number of other Wupatki petroglyphs. In one instance, it is repeated to create an unbounded interlocking band. Were a boundary line present, however, this design would present a typical Sinagua-Salado triangle hook motif. The simple hook is also used in one petroglyph to create a seemingly unique, free-form complex associated with the man (priest?) carrying a hooked cane.

The petroglyphs at Wupatki clearly reflect the Sinagua textile tradition, with few Anasazi influences and with obvious ties to the south and the Hohokam. In prehistoric times, as in many regions of the world today, textiles were popular trade items, and their distinctive designs were copied by the recipients of these goods. For this reason, the designs are sensitive indicators of prehistoric interregional relationships.

All of the above weaving patterns fall into Kent's Late Prehistoric Design category, which is loosely dated between A.D. 1000 and 1400. However, the fact that the Wupatki region was abandoned by about A.D. 1225 restricts the upper limit of the date for the rock art. We can date the petroglyphs more specifically by comparing them with ceramic motifs. The abstract patterns under discussion were not limited to textiles (and petroglyphs); the same combinations of designs were also used to decorate pottery.

The basic structure of the large textile pattern pecked on the edge of North Mesa also decorates Flagstaff Black-on-white vessels (A.D. 1100–1200). Simple hooks and dark solid bands containing negative diamonds with central dots appear on Wupatki Black-on-white (A.D. 1100–1225). Flagstaff Black-on-white and Wupatki Black-on-white vessels also display barbed or sawtooth lines arranged in opposed pairs to create a negative lightning effect similar to that found on textiles and in the rock art. The checkerboard appears at least once at Wupatki as a petroglyph. The checkerboard was a popular Anasazi ceramic motif at this time, but it is less common on Sinagua ceramics. It also occurs as a small decorative design on a Pueblo III basket found in the Wupatki vicinity. Other geometric patterns in Wupatki rock art, such as the interlocking rectilinear scrolls with associated barbed lines, resemble elements on Pueblo II and Pueblo III ceramics dating from A.D. 1070–1225.

These textile and ceramic associations enable us to date the related petroglyph designs and their associated life forms with some degree of confidence within the 160-year period between the eruption of Sunset Crater (A.D. 1065) and the abandonment of the region early in the thirteenth century.

There are suggestions, however, that this time frame does not, in fact, account for all of the rock art in the Wupatki vicinity. For example, the eye-catching outlined cross may have different implications. Although its presence is sporadic, this design is widespread in the rock art of the Southwest, from the Virgin-Kayenta Anasazi region of southeastern Nevada to the Big Bend vicinity in Texas. Also it was used as a pottery motif by both the Anasazi and the Mimbreños, a factor that is useful in dating its appearance on the rocks.

Textiles such as this Sinagua brocaded cotton cloth fragment from a site near Camp Verde, Arizona, may have inspired petroglyphs such as the one on North Mesa near Wupatki. The steep pitch of the main structural lines is reminiscent of Hohokam patterns.

These spirals with extended lines or paths may symbolize migrations, as in Zuni and Hopi interpretations of this motif. Photo by David Noble, 1986.

The simple hooks and solid bands enclosing negative diamonds with central dots in these petroglyphs are common to textiles and ceramic designs in the region. The checkerboard, however, was a popular contemporary Anasazi ceramic design. Photo by David Noble, 1986.

Unbounded limitless textile pattern and ceramic design as a petroglyph on sandstone near Wupatki. Photo by David Noble, 1986.

The outlined cross is particularly prevalent on ceramics from the San Juan region, where it is depicted on late Basketmaker III and Pueblo I ceramics (types include La Plata Black-on-white, A.D. 500–800; Bluff Black-on-red, A.D. 800–900; and especially Piedra Black-on-white, A.D. 750–900). Much more rarely it may appear on a Pueblo II vessel. This element is also found to the south in a poorly dated context among the petroglyphs of the Reserve area, and among Mimbres petroglyphs as well as on Mimbres Black-on-white pottery (A.D. 1050–1150), where it is slightly modified as a negative design. However, its early proliferation as a pottery design element in the Anasazi area is strongly suggestive of a Pueblo I date for its appearance in Wupatki rock art as well. In this event, the outlined cross and associated petroglyphs are perhaps the most visible archaeological manifestation from that period in the Wupatki vicinity because unlike pottery and house remains, the petroglyphs were not covered with cinders during the Sunset Crater eruptions (A.D. 1064–66).

There is a paucity of human figures, animals, birds, and lizards on the ceramics of the Wupatki-Flagstaff region, and they are seemingly completely absent on prehistoric textiles. Mesa Verde ceramics have the most to offer along these lines, yet to compare nuances of figure types on Mesa Verde pottery with those in the distant Sinagua rock art is at best only generally informative. Still, the figure types in Wupatki rock art do broadly conform to contemporary figure representations in the northern Southwest.

The variety of textile/ceramic motifs present in the rock art makes Wupatki petroglyphs a rich source for the cross-media studies touched on here. Why these designs were carved on the rocks in the first place and what meaning they may have held for residents in the Little Colorado River area are questions open to speculation. For example, in Mexico, the equilinear cross has ancient symbolic meaning among the interrelated concepts of the God of Fire, personifications of the Sun, and rays to the four cardinal directions. Ideas derived from Mexican sources may have been present in the Southwest as well.

Unbounded textile pattern of oblique bands offset around interlocking motifs. Photo by David Noble, 1986.

Today and in recent protohistoric rock art, the simple cross usually represents a star. On prehistoric ceramics its use as a strategically placed isolated element suggests that, at a minimum, the outlined cross had aesthetic appeal as a space filler and served a decorative function. On the other hand, in petroglyphs where space filling was not a consideration, the often dominating presence and compelling form of the outlined cross suggests that, in the Southwest as in Mexico, it had specific symbolic meaning when used in the context of life forms, spirals, and other images.

The possible significance of textile designs is also difficult to assess. It is assumed by most archaeologists that small textile patterns casually scratched into the plaster of kiva walls served as "notes" for design layout and details for the weavers, whose looms were set up within. But why were large, intricate patterns laboriously pecked on rocks outside the village confines? Their very location seems to deny that these complicated textile patterns could have served any useful function as weaving guides. Did they have symbolic value? Or did they serve some sort of social purpose? We may never know. In her recent research at Zuni, Jane Young found that her informants responded to similar petroglyphs in two ways: first, like ourselves they recognized them as textile or pottery designs, and second, some regarded them as "done by our ancestors" to communicate "some sort of message that we no longer understand."*

*Mary Jane Young, "Images of Power, Images of Beauty: Contemporary Zuni Perceptions of Rock Art." Dissertation in Folklore and Folklife. University of Pennsylvania, 1982.

Polly Schaafsma is a rock-art specialist and author of Indian Rock Art of the Southwest. *She is also an artist.*

Peshlakai Etsidi, 1936. Photo by Philip Johnston. Courtesy, Museum of Northern Arizona.

The Wupatki Navajos

An Historical Sketch

by Alexandra Roberts

TUBA CITY'S DAMP, dark woolen mill was an old sandstone building that served as a temporary Protestant mission. There in 1897, the Reverend William R. Johnston first met Peshlakai Etsidi, whose Navajo name meant Silversmith. Struck by the Navajo's outstanding appearance and dignified manner, the reverend asked the local trader who Peshlakai Etsidi was.

They tell me he's one of the first who learned to make silver jewelry, from a Mexican over at Keam's Canyon. He lives at Black Point up the Little Colorado River quite a way south of here.... He's an apprentice to a medicine man. The Indians of this area go to him for advice. Middle forties. Young for a Navajo to have as much influence as he has. Probably in a few years they'll call him Hosteen Peshlakai Etsidi, which is like calling him the Honorable Mister Silversmith. He's the kind who becomes a real "hostui," a wise man. These are the ones who have the strongest influence and hold it all their lives.

When Wupatki National Monument was established by presidential proclamation in 1924, the lines that demarcated its boundaries just south of Black Point were drawn over the territory held by Peshlakai Etsidi and his children and grandchildren. Those grandchildren, great-grandchildren, and great-great-grandchildren inhabit the Wupatki Basin to this day, nearly one hundred twenty years after Peshlakai Etsidi first settled it. The Navajo story of Wupatki begins with him.

Peshlakai Etsidi's predecessors first came to the Coconino area between Wupatki and the Grand Canyon during the late eighteenth century, sharing the resources offered by the Coconino Plateau and the Little Colorado River with Havasupai people throughout the first half of the nineteenth century. These early Navajo families were nomadic, traveling over immense areas each year to gain a subsistence based on sheep herding, agriculture, small game hunting, and wild plant gathering. Except for occasional skirmishes with Mexicans, Utes, and Hopis, the Navajos' seasonal travels were uninterrupted until the arrival of the U.S. Army in the early 1860s.

Under the orders of U.S. General James Carleton, in 1863 Colonel Christopher "Kit" Carson launched a military campaign against the Navajos, the ultimate aim of which was to confine the entire Navajo population at Fort Sumner, New Mexico. Males resisting U.S. troops were to be killed, and women and children taken captive. A bounty was set on Navajo livestock, and their crops were to be destroyed. Word of the campaign reached the Coconino area in 1864, and the majority of Navajo families took flight, seeking refuge in the Grand Canyon and other inaccessible locations. The canyon settings of archaeological sites near Wupatki dating to this time suggest the Navajos' defensive position during this traumatic period.

By 1867, faced with starvation, local Navajo leaders convinced the Coconino Navajos to surrender to U.S. troops. Peshlakai Etsidi, then about eleven or twelve years old, along with his family and other families, including that of his future wife, began a 500-mile journey from the Grand Canyon to central New Mexico. The aged and infirm died along the way, and many more died during the years of captivity at Fort Sumner. Not until the utter failure of the "settlement" program in 1868 did Navajo leaders and the government sign a treaty which established the boundaries of a small reservation and allowed the Navajos to return to their homes.

Peshlakai Etsidi returned with his family to the Coconino Plateau in about 1870. Shortly thereafter, Etsidi married and moved to his wife's family home at Black Point, three miles north of Wupatki. During the next two decades, Etsidi and his wife established a family, acquired large herds of livestock, and worked a ten-acre field of corn. Other Navajos also returned to their original homes along

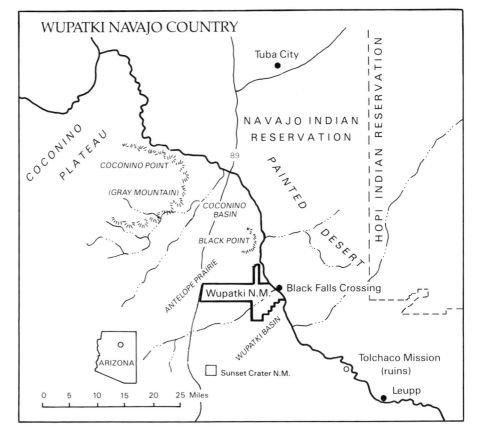

the Little Colorado River and rebuilt their decimated herds of horses and sheep and agricultural fields. Navajo populations spread out east and west of the Little Colorado River, from south of present-day Leupp to the Grand Canyon, including what is now Wupatki.

Before the century was over, Anglo incursions into the far western Navajo territory began again. The year 1876 brought Mormon settlers to the Little Colorado; they established colonies along the length of the river and crossed frequently at Black Falls on Wupatki's eastern border. In 1882, the railroad reached the newly established town of Flagstaff and began bringing pioneering Anglo settlers who would shape the history of the West. The U.S. Government granted the railroad company alternate one-mile-by-one-mile sections for forty miles on either side of the track right-of-way. These railroad sections could be sold by the railroad company or traded for public domain land elsewhere.

Newly arrived Anglo ranchers coveted the scarce water sources and abundant grass on the railroad sections and public domain lands, some of which were occupied by Navajos. By 1897, conflicts had developed. In a typical incident, the board of supervisors of Coconino County, which included local Anglo ranchers, ordered a twenty-man posse to "assess the property" of Navajos in Coconino County. The board demanded a five-dollar tax per 100 head of sheep to be paid immediately by sixteen Navajo families on the Coconino Plateau. The supervisors knew that they would be unable to pay, and when the money was not received, the posse drove both the people and their sheep from their traditional grazing land.

Snow was falling (a deep snow already covered the ground), the weather was bitter cold, and the ewes were lambing. The Indians pleaded for a reasonable time within which to remove, but were denied. Their houses and corrals were burned and they and their flocks were rounded up and pushed toward the Little Colorado River with a relentless haste, the posse keeping women, children and animals in a fright by an intermittent fire from rifles and revolvers. When the river was reached it was found to be so deep to require the sheep to swim. The posse surrounded the flocks and pushed them into the water, and nearly all the lambs, with many grown sheep, went down the stream or chilled to death after crossing, and many died afterward from the effects of exposure. The loss to the Indians was equivalent to several thousand dollars.

A NEGLECTED PEOPLE

"No man sought after my Soul."—Psalm 142: 4. (Margin)

Issued Quarterly.   JANUARY—MARCH, 1903.   Vol. IV. No. 1.

Mr. Johnston and the Two Navajos who accompanied him to Philadelphia and Washington, "She-She-Nez" and "Pesh-la-ki-Etsetty."

THE NAVAJO MISSION.

Report of the Interesting Meeting Recently Held.

The newsletter of Tolchaco Mission, 1903.

Peshlakai Etsidi's family was wintering on the Coconino Plateau that January of 1897. Although offenses against their people had happened before, Etsidi and other influential leaders urged the Navajos not to seek retaliation against the Anglo strangers. Instead, on behalf of the Coconino families, Etsidi traveled to Tuba City to request the assistance of the newly arrived Protestant missionary, Reverend William R. Johnston. Their meeting was the beginning not only of a lifelong friendship, but also of a small influence on Indian/government rela-

At Tolchaco Mission, 1904. Back row, left to right: F. G. Mitchell; Vera Standish, Pesh-lakai's wife; Peshlakai Etsidi; Reverend William R. Johnston; Bwoo Adin, one of the head-men who went to Washington. Middle row: Lizzie Scott, the mission teacher; Mrs. W. R. Johnston; Philip Johnston; David Johnston. Front row: Mary Johnston, La Pah. Courtesy, Museum of Northern Arizona.

tions. Etsidi spoke to Johnston with a power and eloquence that moved Johnston to action on behalf of the Navajo people. "In a way," Johnston remarked in retrospect, "it was like meeting one of the biblical figures, Isaac or Jacob."

Three years later, Reverend Johnston, his wife, and their children, Mary and Philip, moved from Tuba City and established a mission at Tolchaco, about fifteen miles upriver from Wupatki's eastern boundary. In 1902 and 1904, Etsidi accompanied Johnston and other local headmen on two trips to Washington, D.C. There, with young Philip Johnston acting as interpreter, Etsidi presented the story of Navajo hardship to President Theodore Roosevelt. The president listened, and after presenting Etsidi and his companions with medals proclaiming them official leaders of their people, he instituted an immediate program of reservation boundary extensions and Indian allotments in the western territory. Government

land surveyors and alloting agents congregated in the Coconino area during 1908 to conduct land studies for the distribution of allotments and additions to the reservation created by the 1868 treaty. The twenty-four-square-mile Leupp extension, about twenty miles south of Wupatki on the Little Colorado River, was officially added to the reservation. This extension enabled the addition of a school and irrigation projects, as well as the protection of some Navajo grazing range from Anglo ranchers.

Thus, within the first decade of the twentieth century, presidential attention had been drawn to the plight of the Navajos on the public domain in the Wupatki area. But presidential attention turned to the area for other reasons as well. Severe looting of major ruins by local pothunters prompted Dr. Harold S. Colton, founder of the Museum of Northern Arizona, to request government protection of the two largest ruins. Three and a half sections of land were set

aside as Wupatki National Monument under presidential proclamation 1721 on December 9, 1924. Ten years later, the monument received its first full-time custodians, Jimmy and Sally Brewer, who lived in two converted rooms of the ancient Wupatki Pueblo. To cover the forty miles to Flagstaff on dirt track, they used a truck that the National Park Service purchased from the Bureau of Public Roads for $5.00. The Brewers quickly established close friendships with their Navajo neighbors.

The 1930s were rough for the Navajos, as they were for the entire nation. Tuberculosis was rampant, and the local families sacrificed much of their property to paying medicine men who performed curing ceremonies. After each death, the hogan in which the person died was abandoned, according to custom, leaving some families temporarily homeless. The fervor of the 1908 allotting program had subsided, and many government promises remained unful-

Katharine Bartlett, Dr. and Mrs. Will Dakin, and Dr. Colton visiting the Peshlakai family in Wupatki Basin, 1936. Courtesy, Museum of Northern Arizona.

filled. The grazing areas that were left to the Navajos by ranchers were poor and severely overgrazed, and the remaining sheep were unprolific. Yet, despite the lean economic situation, the friendship and mutual respect established between the Brewers and the Navajos brought Anglo/Navajo relations at Wupatki to an all-time high.

The pinnacle of these good relations between the National Park Service and the Navajos occured between the winters of 1935 and 1936, with two legendary Christmas parties and the first Navajo Craftsman Exhibition, now a renowned annual function of the Museum of Northern Arizona. These events involved the Brewers, representing the National Park Service; Dr. and Mrs. Harold S. Colton; Harvard archaeologist Watson Smith; archaeologist Charles Steen; historian and archaeologist Katharine Bartlett; and Philip Johnston and his wife, Bernice; in addition to about forty Navajo

residents of the Wupatki basin, nearly all of whom were Etsidi's children, grandchildren, and in-laws.

It was these events that not only made the Navajo occupants of the Wupatki Basin an integral part of the National Park Service operation but also brought regional attention to this remote corner of Arizona. The Navajo Craftsman Exhibition was held in a specially constructed ceremonial hogan and four large ramadas just north of Wupatki Pueblo. The event required four months of joint preparation by the Brewers, the Coltons, and all of the Navajo residents of the Wupatki Basin. On June 6 and 7, 1936, there were 127 visitors who traveled the forty miles of dirt road from Flagstaff to Wupatki to participate in the significant event.

The show perpetuated knowledge of vanishing traditional arts among the Western Navajo, the effects of which are carried on in the work of today's Navajo artists. It set the stage

for the Museum of Northern Arizona's annual Navajo Craftsman Exhibition, which draws Navajo artists and visitors from around the country and has provided a starting point for many Navajo artists. Most importantly, however, the Navajo show and the two Christmas parties at Wupatki in 1935 and 1936 created the first really successful relationships between the Wupatki Navajos and Anglos since their first contact almost eighty years before. At these functions Peshlakai Etsidi gave his last speeches, urging continued cooperation between the two cultures that had become permanent residents of the same high desert.

Peshlakai Etsidi was buried in the hogan in which he died in April 1939. Before his death, Wupatki National Monument was enlarged from 2,234 acres to nearly 35,000 acres, encompassing the entire Wupatki Basin. Dr. Colton and Philip and Bernice Johnston continued to work for the

Navajos' rights to their traditional homelands, emphasizing the role of the National Park Service in protecting the Navajo culture within Wupatki's boundaries. The Navajos also worked towards the cooperative relationships that Etsidi had urged. During the 1930s and 1940s, for example, Etsidi's son, Clyde Peshlakai, played a fundamental part in Park Service operations. Clyde became Wupatki National Monument's "support staff." He conducted tours; participated in the construction and design of facilities; maintained the grounds; provided the custodians and visitors with folk knowledge of the monument's natural and cultural features; and in 1956 even located a unique geological feature, the blow-hole, near the Wupatki ball court.

By the second half of the 1940s, however, Navajo and Anglo attention turned from local concerns to World War II, in which the Wupatki Navajos indirectly played a significant role. Philip Johnston had learned fluent Navajo while growing up at Tolchaco Mission, and he organized the Navajo Code Talkers in 1942, forty years after

Descendants of Peshlakai Etsidi. Left to right, Della Yazzie, a granddaughter; Helen Davis, a great-granddaughter; Stella Smith, Helen's mother and Della's sister; and three great-great-grandsons, Aaron, Tony, and Myron Davis. Photo by Alexandra Roberts, 1987.

Clyde Peshlakai, acting custodian at Wupatki National Monument, 1936. Photo by Jim Brewer. Courtesy, Museum of Northern Arizona.

interpreting the conversations between President Roosevelt and Peshlakai Etsidi. Using a code language based on Navajo, the Code Talkers played a significant role in U.S. military communications during World War II. "Considering the remarkable fact," wrote Johnston during the war, "that we have the only system of air-tight, secret communication by voice-radio, I have every reason to believe that the Navajos will make real history before we are finished." Johnston's prediction proved correct.

The Wupatki Navajos fought in the war as well, and many young men enlisted in the army to serve the nation, less than eighty years after the U.S. Army had imprisoned their grandparents at Fort Sumner. The war was far from Wupatki, but it hit close to home as Navajo mothers and fathers asked the superintendent of the monument to write letters to their sons stationed in foreign places of which they had never heard.

Increasing governmental bureaucracy following the war years eventually strained relations between the

Navajos and the National Park Service. By the early 1960s, all Navajo families except that of Clyde Peshlakai had moved off the monument. Clyde died in 1970 and is buried in the rock house just north of monument headquarters, off the monument highway. Today, his offspring—third, fourth, and fifth generation descendants of the original Navajo settlers—continue nearly one hundred twenty years of Navajo heritage within Wupatki's boundaries. Wupatki National Monument protects the numerous archaeological remains of this long Navajo occupation. The archaeological record represents five generations of a Navajo family whose experience at Wupatki reflects not only the course of local events but also broader manifestations of the American Indian role in the nation's history.

Alexandra Roberts is on the staff of the Navajo Nation Archaeology Department.

WALNUT CANYON

A View into the Past

by Pat H. Stein and Anne R. Baldwin

Visitors to Walnut Canyon, ca. 1890. Courtesy, Northern Arizona Pioneers Historical Society, Northern Arizona University.

Explorers and Pothunters

BEFORE SCIENTISTS OF THE SMITHSONIAN Institution "discovered" Walnut Canyon in 1883, Flagstaff residents knew its ruins well. Located only nine miles from a settlement on the Atlantic and Pacific Railroad line, the Sinagua cliff dwellings had become, by the early 1880s, a popular destination for Sunday picnics, club outings, and treasure hunting. By 1940, the legacy of sixty years of pothunting could be seen everywhere: in toppled walls, ransacked rooms, and disturbed archaeological deposits. So severe was the damage that it prompted one archaeologist to write that Walnut Canyon was "a monument to vandalism."

The ancient houses of the wild cliff were a source of delight and mystery to townsfolk such as lumber magnate Michael J. Riordan, who perhaps did more to publicize Walnut Canyon than any other person in the nineteenth century. A tuberculosis patient, Riordan recuperated from his illness by taking leisurely day trips to local points of interest. When John Wesley Powell and James Stevenson of the Smithsonian explored Walnut Canyon in the summer of 1885, Riordan accompanied them and then revisited the ruins ten times in the following four months. Riordan reported his explorations to journals and newspapers throughout the United States, thus promoting the ruins to the scientific and lay communities. He wrote that "the old and silent houses" were in a good state of preservation and that "centuries of storms and adverse circumstances [had] failed to make any appreciable impressions of decay on their exposed fronts." Riordan's writings revealed his obvious pride in the fruits of pothunting:

> Innumerable pieces of...pottery are scattered around the dwellings, but it is fast being carried off by scientists and curiosity hunters. However, I think I have the largest and finest collection of it to be found.

As the reputation of Walnut Canyon grew, travelers from far away often included it in their itineraries. Through brochures and trackside billboards the railroad promoted such visitation and also conducted tours starting from its siding at Cliffs. One woman who took advantage of such a travel package reported her Walnut Canyon foray to the *San Francisco Call*:

> It is very dusty work to dig for relics, especially if the room has only a slight opening. If it were not for this dryness, however, the relics would not have been so well preserved....We dug for an hour or more, and found, among other things, an old stone mill (metate and mano),...cornstalks, corncobs in abundance, beans, gourds, uncracked nuts, reeds, arrows, bowstrings,...coarse cloth, a child's sandal, a measuring stick with notches at regular intervals, smoothly worn sticks of hard wood, bone needles, a fish line, soapweed needles, broken pottery, etc. In visiting other dwellings we added to these relics, and came away heavily laden.

Looters sometimes resorted to more extreme measures to dig at the cliff dwellings. Dynamite was used to blast the front walls so that pothunters would have more light and room in which to work.

By the 1890s, Flagstaff residents were awakening to the facts that the cliff dwellings had economic value as tourist attractions and that these attractions were rapidly being destroyed. An 1891 meeting of the Flagstaff Board of Trade (forerunner of the Chamber of Commerce) denounced "the mutilation of the Cliff Dwellers' ruins" but took no action to protect them. Visitation increased and the disturbance continued. In 1895, three Flagstaff adventurers reported that they were able to find their way to the ruins simply by following the trail of broken beer bottles. In some places the glass was inches deep, and it was particularly abundant in ruins where visitors camped.

Preservation Efforts

No formal steps were taken to protect Walnut Canyon until the creation of the San Francisco Mountain Forest Reserve. Administered by the Bureau of Forestry (later the U.S. Forest Service), the reserve placed a ranger in charge

of the ruins beginning in 1904. The first ranger was William Henry Pierce, a Civil War veteran who remained at Walnut Canyon until 1921.

Ranger Pierce's strategy in protecting the ruins was one of gentle persuasion, even after passage of the 1906 Antiquities Act. Pierce suspected that antiquities were leaving the canyon in picnic baskets but did not search for concealed artifacts for fear of offending visitors. The elderly ranger, who was sixty-three in 1904, rarely accompanied hikers along the trail, which led from his cabin down Ranger Canyon, then east along Walnut Canyon to Third Fort. "When Pierce was not watching, [visitors] would sneak around a few other places," an oldtimer recalled. Ranger Pierce's effectiveness in protecting the ruins was further eroded by the fact that he held only a seasonal position; pothunters struck during his absence.

By the 1910s, Flagstaff leaders saw that the future prosperity of their town would depend largely on the tourist trade, and Walnut Canyon was a key element in that trade. Distinctive among such leaders was Father Cyprian Vabre, a Roman Catholic priest who urged protection of the ruins on moral as well as economic grounds. Vabre warned his parish that "to vandalize Walnut Canyon is to desecrate a Holy Place." Through his friendship with President Theodore Roosevelt and other national leaders, Vabre continually focused attention on the need to preserve Walnut Canyon and other scenic wonders of the Southwest. Moreover, Vabre was vice-president of the Good Roads Association and the Parks-to-Parks Highway Association. Insisting that "wherever good roads go, Christianity follows as a matter of course," he successfully lobbied to have the National Ocean-to-Ocean Highway routed through northern Arizona. Thus a visit to Walnut Canyon became only a short detour from a major transcontinental road.

Ranger Pierce in front of the old ranger cabin. Courtesy, Northern Arizona Pioneers Historical Society, Northern Arizona University.

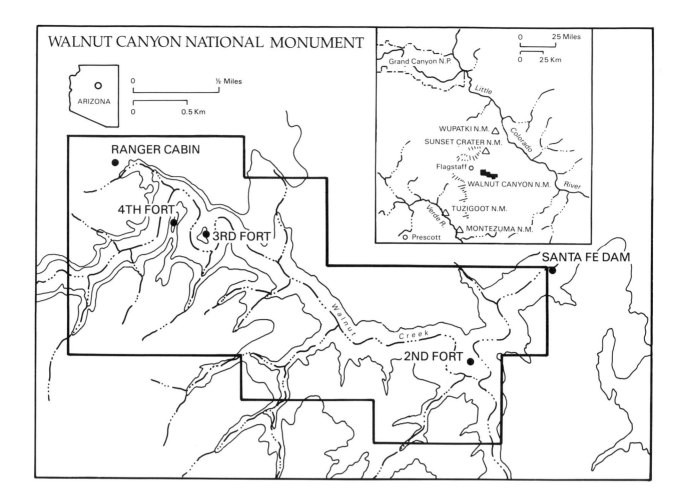

WALNUT CANYON NATIONAL MONUMENT

ARIZONA

0   ½ Miles

0   0.5 Km

RANGER CABIN

4TH FORT

3RD FORT

Walnut

Creek

2ND FORT

SANTA FE DAM

0   25 Miles

0   25 Km

Grand Canyon N.P.

Little

WUPATKI N.M.

SUNSET CRATER N.M.

Flagstaff

WALNUT CANYON N.M.

Colorado

River

TUZIGOOT N.M.

Verde R.

MONTEZUMA N.M.

Prescott

The campaign to make Walnut Canyon a national monument grew as a grassroots movement of the 1910s. On July 14, 1915, the Daughters of the American Revolution installed on the Ocean-to-Ocean Highway near Walnut Canyon a plaque honoring pioneering women. Dignitaries attending the ceremony—including Arizona Governor George Hunt —were presented with a petition signed by Flagstaff residents requesting the establishment of a national monument at the cliff dwellings. The drive was successful, and on November 30, 1915, Woodrow Wilson issued a presidential proclamation creating Walnut Canyon National Monument.

Most national monuments were transferred from the U.S. Forest Service to the National Park Service in 1916, but Walnut Canyon remained under Forest Service control for eighteen more years. During that time the Forest Service made many improvements at the monument: it repaired trails, kept the ruins free of trash, and installed ladders that allowed visitors to climb from lower to upper levels of some cliff dwellings.

Also during the Forest Service era the ruins became the focus of scholarly study by Dr. Harold Sellers Colton. A professor of zoology at the University of Pennsylvania, Colton first visited Walnut Canyon in 1912, while honeymooning with his bride, Mary-Russell Ferrell. The couple became intrigued with northern Arizona and returned

yearly to study its ruins and natural wonders. Encouraged by Jesse Walter Fewkes of the Smithsonian Institution, Colton undertook an archaeological survey of Walnut Canyon in the late 1910s and early 1920s. In 1926, the Coltons moved to Flagstaff and founded the Museum of Northern Arizona (MNA). Six years later Dr. Colton and MNA colleague Lyndon Hargrave completed the first professional excavation and stabilization of a Walnut Canyon ruin, site NA 739.

When Walnut Canyon National Monument was transferred from the U.S. Forest Service to the National Park Service in 1934, Colton urged the Park Service to place a trained archaeologist in charge of the ruins. Southwestern Monuments Superintendent Frank ("The Boss") Pinckley responded by appointing as ranger Paul Beaubien, an archaeologist with extensive experience in the western United States. Beaubien championed the protection and development of the monument with a tenacity that earned him the respect of the archaeological community and the general public. He patrolled the trail frequently and tried to instill a conservation ethic in each visitor. No longer could the visitor pocket interesting objects, for Beaubien did not hesitate to question suspicious-looking tourists and demand that pilfered artifacts be returned.

Operating with extremely limited funding and manpower, Beaubien found that each step forward was countered by one backward. He was the only Park Service employee usually stationed at the monument, and he simply could not contact and monitor all visitors. He also spent much of his time dealing with bovine intrusions; the canyon was not fenced, and cattle roamed freely in the ruins, causing the collapse of many walls.

The catalytic event that instigated improvement of the situation at Walnut Canyon was expansion of the monument in order to include the ranger cabin and Second Fort within the boundaries. The Park Service agreed that after these additions, it would develop trails, construct buildings, and enhance the cultural resources of the monument. The expansion was granted in 1938 by President Franklin D. Roosevelt, and the monument was enlarged to its present size of 1,920 acres.

The Park Service soon laid the groundwork for improving Walnut Canyon National Monument by creating a Civilian Conservation Corps (CCC) camp to serve Walnut Canyon, Wupatki, and Sunset Crater national monuments. CCC labor enabled Beaubien to implement projects he had long planned. Some CCC men were detailed to work as guides, so that the rate of visitor contact increased and the ruins became better protected. The "Three-C Boys" made split rails and, by 1940, had begun to fence the monument. A series of CCC improvements changed the routes of canyon access to the system that visitors enjoy today. A stepped trail was constructed from Observation Point directly down to the Island Trail around Third Fort, and a visitor center was built at the head of the trail. When archaeologist Paul Ezell stabilized three canyon ruins in 1940, CCC men comprised his crew. Even after the CCC was disbanded in 1942, the Park Service continued to fund or otherwise encourage projects that would recover scientific data from the ruins and aid in their preservation.

Between 1940 and 1985, archaeologists have conducted seventeen studies at the monument, ranging from surveys to stabilization and excavation projects. Current knowledge of Walnut Canyon's prehistory is thus based on the painstaking work of many archaeologists, including Colton, Hargrave, Ezell, Raymond Rixey, Roland Richert, Sallie Van Valkenburgh, Robert Euler, Norman Ritchie, Roger Kelly, Martin Mayer, Ed Sudderth, Patricia Gilman, and most recently, Anne Baldwin and Michael Bremer.

Archaeologists have now completely surveyed the north and south rims and have examined much of the canyon. Studies have recorded a total of 242 sites, ranging from artifact scatters without architecture to large, multiroomed dwellings. At the ransacked cliff dwellings, archaeologists were able to salvage some remnants of cultural deposits. Excavators stabilized many of the walls seen today by visitors. Often the studies uncovered disheartening reminders of the era when the dwellings were poorly protected, such as Rixey's 1948 discovery of dynamite fuses in the cliff dwelling walls that he was stabilizing. Gone were many of the perishable remains that looters had taken from rockshelters. However, more promising results came from sites on both rims of the canyon. Archaeologists found that because pothunters' tunnel vision had focused their attention on cliff dwellings they had overlooked equally important, although less spectacular, sites on the rims. Undisturbed ruins remained on both rims of the canyon.

The Canyon's Prehistory

What, then, have such studies revealed about the prehistoric peoples of Walnut Canyon? Archaeologists believe that the earliest human forays into the canyon were seasonal and sporadic. Preceramic hunters and gatherers likely hunted in the ponderosa pine forests and made excursions into the lower elevation woodlands to collect piñon nuts. Such hunter-gatherers left no structures or hearths at Walnut Canyon; their presence is evidenced only by one projectile point, a type referred to as *Pinto*, dating to about 6000 B.C.

Archaeological studies confirmed that the main prehistoric occupants of Walnut Canyon were a group that Colton termed the *Sinagua*. These people are identified archaeologically by a constellation of traits, including the presence of a fine-paste pottery called Alameda Brownware. Although the Sinagua first appeared around A.D. 500

Paul Beaubien on Island Trail. Courtesy, Walnut Canyon National Monument.

to 700 in the Flagstaff area, they apparently did not occupy the monument until around A.D. 800 to 900, and only one site dating to this period has been found. Located on the lower south rim, where soils are deeper and piñon-juniper trees abound, this site consists of an artifact scatter and probable pithouses. Its Sinagua occupants probably harvested readily available seeds and plants and moved away after several seasons.

It appears that Walnut Canyon was not occupied during the period A.D. 900 to 1100. The reasons for this hiatus are puzzling, for many sites dating to this period occur just east of the monument, near Winona. Perhaps the Sinagua found environmental conditions more favorable to the east during the tenth and eleventh centuries.

During the Elden Phase, about A.D. 1150 to 1225, the monument was reinhabited by the Sinagua and underwent its densest occupation. Sinagua presence is most obvious in the cliff dwellings that line the limestone ledges. Formed by deposition from an ancient Permian sea, these ledges lost their more soluble materials to erosion as Wal-

nut Creek wound its way to the west. Within the canyon, archaeologists have recorded over 300 rooms distributed among 87 clusters of sites beneath these rock overhangs.

The cliff dwellers incorporated natural features of the ledges into their rooms. Mud-mortared limestone slabs, still visible in many dwellings, formed the front and side walls. A layer of clay was placed on the rough, irregular limestone surface to produce a smooth floor. Little holes near the juncture of the walls and ceiling vented smoke, and small doorways permitted access. On blackened ceilings, in the soot from countless fires, vandals later carved their initials.

Both the south and, in particular, the north rims of Walnut Canyon were also occupied by Elden Phase Sinagua. By far the most common features on the rims are the one- to two-room fieldhouses, a type of shelter believed to have been used seasonally for agricultural pursuits. Ninety-five such sites occur on the north rim, while thirty-seven occur on the south rim. Fieldhouses are small (usually less than 10 square meters); they are constructed

Walnut Canyon, showing cliff dwellings under ledges. Photo by Paul Logsdon, 1986.

Crew studying south rim cliff structure. Photo by Anne Baldwin, 1987.

of limestone slabs, often are arranged with an opening to the east, and have walls that originally stood about a meter high.

Archaeologists see patterns in the way that sites are distributed across the Walnut Canyon landscape, and these arrangements often suggest ideas about site function. On the north rim, fieldhouses are associated with large multi-room dwellings called pueblos. The pueblos usually represent permanent habitations, and at Walnut Canyon such sites were probably supported by the agricultural products associated with the seasonal fieldhouses. The pattern of south rim sites is different: the pueblos are not present there, and the fieldhouses are more widely scattered. Perhaps the Sinagua felt no need of large habitation sites on the south rim but hoped to use the land there as efficiently as possible. Thus they established fieldhouses to attempt crop production in a different microenvironment.

The Walnut Canyon Forts

Among the important Elden Phase Sinagua sites at Walnut Canyon are unusual features called "forts" because of their relative inaccessability. Five forts occur in the canyon, although only three of them—Second, Third, and Fourth Forts—are located within monument boundaries.

Each fort is connected to the rim by means of a narrow, rocky peninsula of land, and each is believed to have formed a community with other nearby sites. Fieldhouses and pueblos perhaps functioned as support communities for fort occupants and canyon dwellers. The forts may in turn have served as focal points for social and economic activities, such as ceremonies and trade. The locations of the forts suggest that they may have been regulatory posts controlling entry to and exit from the canyon during times of stress when the management of local resources was crucial.

The cluster of sites that comprises Third Fort contains a large room on a limestone bench beneath the top of Third Fort Island. This enclosure is similar in size to Sinagua "community rooms" or gathering places such as the one at Elden Pueblo. Its size and location make it unique at Walnut Canyon. It is difficult to assign a function to this feature, however, because like all of Walnut Canyon's forts, it has never been excavated.

The site groupings described above are important because they tell us how the Sinagua at Walnut Canyon organized their communities and used their land. The resulting settlement patterns yield a picture of the group's organizational abilities, level of social complexity, and relationships within the group and with their neighbors.

Wall connecting Second Fort, seen top left, and North Rim. Photo by Anne Baldwin, 1987.

Conclusions

What can we conclude about the Sinagua people who inhabited Walnut Canyon? They possessed organizational skills that permitted them to make efficient use of available resources. The data suggest a level of social complexity sufficient to produce hierarchical arrangements of people and sites, with status or power conferred on certain individuals within the system.

We also know that the Walnut Canyon Sinagua were part of a much larger system of prehistoric activity in the Flagstaff area. Modern visitors tend to see the ruins as frozen in time and space within the artificial confines of the monument fence; however, in their day the sites were not isolated but rather were part of a larger network of communities and people. During the occupation of Walnut Canyon, distant sites such as Elden Pueblo and Turkey Hills to the northwest also were constructed and occupied. Wupatki Pueblo to the north was a settled and flourishing community. Large habitation sites to the south in the Verde Valley and Red Rock country—Montezuma Castle, Honanki, Palatki, and parts of Tuzigoot—were built.

The eleventh through thirteenth centuries in the Southwest were times of great change and transition. Studies indicate that climatic fluctuations produced alternating wet and dry periods that had profound effects on the land, the animals, and the people. By A.D. 1300 the Sinagua had left Walnut Canyon and many other nearby areas. If we think of the canyon not as an isolated instance, but as part of a larger process, we are better able to view southwestern prehistory as a dynamic interaction between many cultural groups and their environment.

Did the Park Service arrive at Walnut Canyon too late to conserve its archaeologial sites? It appears not. The damaged but spectacular cliff dwellings still draw the attention of more than 90,000 visitors annually, and the intact, protected deposits of rim sites will beckon archaeologists for generations to come. The relatively undisturbed rim sites constitute a potential warehouse of information on how the Walnut Canyon Sinagua used their land and conducted their lives. Further excavation and study will help us understand the social and environmental factors that affected the Sinagua of the Flagstaff area.

Pat H. Stein and Anne R. Baldwin, staff archaeologists of Coconino National Forest in Flagstaff, Arizona, authored reports in Walnut Canyon: An Archaeological Survey, *published in 1986 by the Western Archaeological Conservation Center.*

Other titles on the National Parks of the Southwest:

Understanding the Anasazi of Mesa Verde and Hovenweep, edited by David Grant Noble

Pecos Ruins, edited by David Grant Noble

Salinas, edited by David Grant Noble

Zuni and El Morro, edited by David Grant Noble

Houses Beneath the Rock: The Anasazi of Canyon de Chelly and Navajo National Monument, edited by David Grant Noble

The Magic of Bandelier, by David E. Stuart

For further information on current prices and shipping charges, please contact:

Ancient City Press
P.O. Box 5401
Santa Fe, New Mexico 87502
(505) 982-8195